Unsolicited Advice My Grief, My Rules

By:

Tracey Crump

ISBN 9798272206725

Dedication

In loving memory of India Kinamore. Your memory remains forever in our hearts.

Author's Note

This book is based on the true story of my life. I have taken some creative steps to turn it into a story that both honors my experience and protects my family's privacy. The grief you will read about is real.

Losing my two sons, Michael and Steve, broke me in ways I am still trying to understand. The sadness, the anger, and the slow climb back toward purpose all come directly from my own journey through loss.

Although my family is larger and includes more children, I have daughters as well as sons, each of my children carries their own pain, strength, and story.

I wrote it to share how I learned to live again after loss. Too many families know this kind of loss. Too many mothers sit in silence, wondering what they missed. Too many siblings grow up too soon, trying to hold everyone together.

If my words can reach even one person who feels lost in their grief, help one family start talking about mental health, or remind one parent that healing is possible even after the unthinkable, then sharing my story will have been worth it.

This book is my truth, born from love, shaped by loss, and offered in hope.

Table of Contents

Chapter 1: Moonlight in the Rain

In the quiet corners of Cincinnati, the rain cast a melodic rhythm against the window, each drop a bittersweet reminder of Tracey's heartache. Shadows danced across the dimly lit living room, where laughter had once thrived but now lingered only as echoes of memory. Just hours ago, the world outside was a swirl of grey, mirroring the heavy cloud over her heart.

It had been only one day since she had received the call, the knock that shattered her universe. The police officer stood at her door, gravity etched into his face. With a voice like lead, he delivered the news of Michael's passing. An endless loop of disbelief replayed in her mind, drowning out the familiar sounds of the house. "No," she thought, "not again." The ghosts of grief had picked up familiar patterns; this was not her first encounter with loss.

Twelve years ago, it had been Steve, her firstborn, whose laughter filled the halls and whose dreams had brightened their lives. A freak accident — a miscalculated turn, a moment's distraction — had stolen him away too soon. Tracey had thought the waves of grief would recede, that time might soothe the jagged edges of loss. She had cultivated the memories of Steve lovingly, preserving them as relics of a bygone era. But now, just as she had begun to find a flicker of peace, Michael had vanished, leaving silence anew.

As the rain poured steadily, Tracey wrapped her arms tightly around her knees, seeking solace in a moment's reprieve. Michael had been her sunshine — a boy with dreams of space exploration and inventions that could change the world. She could still see his tousled brown hair and the way his eyes sparkled with endless curiosity. Oh, how she would give anything to hear him shout, "Mom! You won't believe what I discovered today!" But on this rain-soaked evening, the echoes of him were drowned out by the grief looming large.

She tried to gather her thoughts, sifting through fragments of memories like leaves scattering in the wind. A game of basketball in the driveway, late-night stargazing in the backyard, guitar strings strummed softly against the backdrop of a setting sun — but those pictures felt tarnished against the brutal reality of loss.

Then, amidst the storm inside her, something broke through: the framed photo on the mantle. It was a vibrant snapshot of their last family trip — the three of them: her, Steve, and Michael — smiling against a sunset backdrop, arms draped over each other's shoulders, a moment frozen in lacquered glass, untouched by time.

Tracey rose, her heart heavy, and crossed the room. She pulled the frame close, tracing the outlines of her beloved boys with trembling fingers. "I don't know how to do this, my loves — how to keep your flames alive in a world that feels so dark without you," she whispered, as if her words could reach them and bridge the chasm death had created.

With the rain continuing its soft lament, an unexpected sense of clarity began to blossom alongside the pain. Maybe the beauty of memory, however sharp, could coexist with the ache of loss. She struggled to pull herself from the weight of despair, feeling instead a rise of determination — she could honor Michael's brilliance, just as she had done for Steve.

As tears mingled with the rain outside, Tracey moved to the dining room table, pulling out paper and pens, blank canvases waiting for life. She began to write, pouring her heart onto the pages: stories of Michael's dreams, sketches of his wild inventions, and the laughter they had shared. She penned the things she wished she could tell him — the things that had slipped beneath the surface of everyday life.

As she wrote, the rain slowed, its rhythm softening as if in response to her cathartic release. She fell deeper into the pages, captivated not just by loss but by the triumph of memory — the way love transcends absence. In this act of creation, she began to piece together the narrative of her life with her boys, honoring the stories of their laughter, their dreams, their light.

With night deepening outside, Tracey sat back, weary but resolute, surrounded by the ink-stained pages that had breathed life anew into her memories. She understood, in that quiet moment, that though the world had dimmed, her love would be an unwavering beacon, lighting the path for both Michael and Steve, forever intertwined in her heart.

The rain had finally ceased, and as the clouds parted, glimmers of moonlight spilled softly into the room, illuminating the remnants of her past and the fragile hopes for her future. In Cincinnati, on that quiet night, Tracey began to understand that grief, while heavy and unyielding, could be shaped into something new.

Chapter 2: Flicker of Hope

The wind whispered through the trees, a haunting lament that seemed to echo Tracey's sorrow. She stood at the edge of the grave, a small mound of earth that marked the end of Michael's journey. As the sun dipped below the horizon, painting the sky with strokes of crimson and violet, she felt as if the universe had conspired against her, deciding that two should be the limit of her blessings, and now, two were buried beneath the soil of her despair.

Michael had always been the light in her life, his laughter ringing like a melody through their modest home. His spirit was electric, sparking joy even in the darkest moments. But that brightness had dimmed over the past year, shadows creeping in where once there was unyielding sunshine. Tracey had sensed the shift, the way his laughter sometimes faltered, replaced by a distant look in his eyes. Yet every time she reached out, he would smile that same smile and say, "I'm fine, Mom. Just tired."

It wasn't until the day she found a crumpled note in the dark recesses of his backpack that the truth slapped her across the face — a plea for help hidden beneath layers of silence. The words "I can't do this anymore" haunted her like a ghost. It wasn't enough to revitalize the deadened hope in her heart. She tried to reach him, tried to bridge the gaps between them, but it felt like grasping at smoke that vanished whenever she got too close.

Now, standing by the grave, her heart felt like it was being compressed into a tiny, hopeless sphere. She thought of her first son, Steve, whose laughter still echoed in dreams, a child so full of life, taken too soon by an illness that had come out of nowhere. The world had grown dark the day she lost Steve, but now, with Michael gone, it felt as if all light had completely evaporated.

She dropped to her knees, the cold earth biting against her skin, and all the memories came flooding back: Michael's first steps, his first words, the way he would sit on her lap, his head resting against her chest as she read him bedtime stories. Each memory was a stab to her heart, each laugh a knife twisted further.

Tears streamed down her face, mingling with the dry earth beneath her palms. "Why?" she whispered, her voice trembling in the air. "Why did you leave me?" The emptiness echoed her words back, leaving only silence as a reply.

As she cried, she felt something shift within her. The weight on her chest, the suffocating darkness, began to morph into a different kind of pain — one that demanded to be shared, to be transformed. She remembered a conversation they'd had not long before he left. They had talked about how the world felt so heavy sometimes, and he'd said, "If I could just show everyone how dark it gets, I think they'd understand."

In that moment, she realized that she could honor Michael by sharing his story, by pulling back the curtain of silence that surrounded mental health, by making sure other families knew they were not alone, that they could reach out and ask for help. She knew that if she could get through the darkness — if she could bear this pain — then maybe, just maybe, she could help someone else.

As she stood to leave, she took a deep breath, tasting the bittersweet air tinged with impending night. She looked back one last time at the grave, whispering, "I will remember you, Michael. I will fight for you, for all the lights that are flickering. I will not let the darkness win."

With renewed resolve, she turned away from the mounds of grief and chose to walk toward a future where her pain could transform into purpose. Though the journey ahead would be long and riddled with heartache, she felt a flicker of hope stirring within her — a fragile flame, but a flame nonetheless. And for now, that was enough.

Chapter 3: Rituals of Remembrance

In the days following Michael's funeral, the sun poured through the kitchen window, casting warm light on the faded checkered tablecloth that had covered the table they'd shared for nearly a decade. Tracey stood there, her hands busily arranging the flowers — a mismatched bouquet of wildflowers and white lilies that felt both beautiful and out of place in the stillness of the house. She could almost hear his voice echoing through the rooms, teasing her about her penchant for chaos.

"Why do you need all those flowers, Trace? They'll just wilt!" he had joked.

But now, the colors seemed to mock her sorrow, vibrant against her muted grief. "This can't be happening," she whispered, the words escaping her lips like a prayer. She looked at the flowers as if they held the power to conjure him back, but all they offered was the hollow scent of inevitability.

Cleaning spaces that felt too empty, she traced her fingers across the dust-laden surfaces, her movements mechanical — a ritual designed to stave off despair. Each stroke of the cloth was a whisper of denial, a cocoon of unyielding hope wrapping around her fragile heart. The kitchen held echoes of laughter, fridge magnets shaped like silly animals holding photos of vacations and birthday celebrations. But in their stillness, they offered only reflections of what once was — no new memories would ever grace these walls.

She wandered from room to room, caught in a labyrinth of reminiscences. The living room held their shared dreams — the faded sofa where they binge-watched shows after long days, where they celebrated anniversaries with takeout and laughter over clinking glasses. The absence of Michael felt like a gaping wound where warmth once thrived.

Instinctively, she moved to the bookshelf, brushing her fingers along the lined spines of his favorite novels, lingering on *The Old Man and the Sea*. It had been his staple read, a reminder of resilience. With the book in hand, she sank into the worn leather armchair — the one he had claimed as his with a simple, possessive nod one cool autumn evening — letting the familiar scent of aged pages wrap around her.

As dusk approached, shadows stretched across the floor, and Tracey felt the weight of the day settling in her bones. She glanced at the clock; time seemed an old foe, taunting her with its relentless march forward.

She pulled out her phone, her fingers hovering over a photo of Michael mid-laugh, a slice of pizza dangling from his mouth. It was absurd, yet so quintessentially him. She hesitated for just a moment before sharing it on social media — a bold act of remembrance that felt both liberating and terrifying. "Love you, forever," she typed, her heart heavy but full of unspoken words, each letter a step toward someone she feared forgetting.

The following days merged into a fog, a cycle of ordinary tasks that numbed her senses. But one evening, as she sorted through their old board games, a bright red box caught her eye — *Exploding Kittens*. It was opened but never played. Michael had insisted they start at least one game night a month; she could hear his playful insistence echoing within the silent room.

An idea sparked, fueling a flicker of life within her. With the game spread across the dining table, she set out a bottle of wine and two glasses — a cheerful act steeped in nostalgia. She poured the wine and raised her glass, a toast made only to the memory that filled the empty spaces in her heart.

"Here's to you, Michael. To all our games yet to be played," she whispered into the silence, a ghostly audience absorbing her words.

Surprisingly, the nightly ritual of game night became a balm for her raw grief. Over days and weeks, she invited friends and family for laughter and connection — a small community rekindling the warmth that had dimmed so suddenly. The games, the laughter, the missed jests — it began to ease the weight of loss, though the scars lingered.

As the holidays approached and the first snow fell, Tracey decorated the house alone but with intention, twinkling lights wrapping around the staircase. She held onto his spirit, letting every ornament remind her of him — a blue star to represent their first Christmas together, a little snowman from their last trip.

On Christmas Eve, she placed three stockings by the fire — one for herself and another for Michael and Steve— filled with little mementos: a "Wish You Were Here" postcard, an old candy cane, and his number one jersey from his high school basketball days.

That night, she sat by the fire, gazing at the flickering flames as they danced and swirled. She could almost feel him beside her, his laughter resonating like a distant echo. "You always took too long to decorate," he'd tease. "But I'll let you have a pass this time."

Chapter 4: From Fury to Flame

Tracey stood at the edge of Eden Park, her fists clenched and her heart pounding like war drums in her chest. The view below was breathtaking — a tapestry of wildflowers dancing in the warm breeze and the calm waves of the ocean rolling in rhythm with life. But she saw none of it. Instead, her gaze was locked on the horizon, where sharp shadows of the mountains loomed like mighty giants. They seemed to mirthlessly watch her internal battle, each breath an agonizing reminder of her family's misfortune.

"Why them and not me?" she shouted, her voice breaking against the wind. Unleashed, her fury surged through her veins, twisting and turning into something potent and wild. She felt like a caged beast, wrestling with the invisible bars of a cruel fate that had decided to toy with her family — a family she wished had been spared. In her mind, chaotic images of her mother's recent tears and her father's weary sighs piled atop each other like a deluge, drowning her in despair.

Anger lit her insides like a spark igniting a cannon. "Why do you take them?" she spat at the heavens, her words echoing violently against the rocks that anchored the cliff. Her hands trembled as she imagined the countless times her family had gathered, laughing and sharing stories until the sun dipped below the horizon. They knew hardships too, but this — this was an unbearable weight that made the air feel thick and suffocating.

"Why is everyone moving on as if nothing happened?" she yelled, her voice tapering into a feral growl. Friends who reached out to comfort her felt the lash of her tongue instead. They were bewildered; they didn't understand the hollowness she was navigating. "You don't know!" she barked at Tanika one afternoon, and she could see her friend's lovely face turn pale with hurt.

Mary, her best friend since grade school, stood frozen in shock. "Tracey — I'm just trying to help," she whispered, her voice soft and trembling.

"Help? By telling me everything will be okay? Nothing is okay!" She could feel her words lacerate the air between them like a knife. The guilt settled in her stomach, coiling around the anger like a serpent, but she could not retract her words. The world continued to breathe seamlessly, with people giggling as they passed by their café and sunlight bleeding through the clouds like nothing touched them at all.

Days morphed into nights, and her anger, mixed with betrayal, summoned storms within her. Friends faded away, unable to navigate the tempest that had become Tracey. And yet, it wasn't only loss driving her wrath; it was the insistent ache of loneliness that fed her rage. She felt like a lone wolf, howling atop a mountain, demanding recognition from a world that had plunged into apathy.

One gray evening, as rain began to wash away her barriers, it became clear that she could no longer barricade herself in rage. So, she visited the old oak tree by the shore — their family tree, where she and her siblings had played as children. Its gnarled bark felt familiar beneath her fingers, a heart beating in perpetual silence. Kneeling before it, she pressed her forehead onto the trunk, feeling its solidity grounding her.

"I'm angry," she confessed into the fading light, "I'm so angry that they're gone, and I'm still here, stuck in a life without them." The thunder rolled overhead, mirroring her heart's tumult. "It isn't fair!"

As the raindrops began to drench her hair, something changed in the quiet moment. She allowed the anger to flow through her now, not as a destructive force, but like a river that needed to find its way home. Each patter against the earth seemed to soften her heart rather than harden it. In the midst of her fury lay an unexpected passion, her love for her family, a fire that would not be extinguished.

At that moment, the sky split and the clouds surrendered, and with it came clarity. Tracey realized anger was only a chapter in her story, one that, like storms, would pass. And despite the chasms of loss, she could use that fury as fuel, igniting a path not just for her healing but a tribute to her family's memory, a fierce reminder that they had lived fiercely and deserved to be honored.

Later that night, she began to write. Words flowed about laughter from the house, echoed by hearts that beat a rhythm of love beneath the sunlight. A tribute to all that they had been and all that they would forever be in her heart. Tracey had found a way to transform anger's fury into something beautiful, a storm settling into serenity, a beginning woven from her family's enduring love.

Chapter 5: Weaving Hope from Sorrow

Tracey stood in the dim light of her living room, the walls a faded reminder of laughter and chaos that once filled the space. The room was a gallery of shadowy memories, photos, drawings, trophies adorned the mantle, each piece a fragment of a life that felt like a distant dream. Each night, the heartache wrapped around her like a heavy blanket, the fabric of which was woven with "what ifs" and "if onlys."

Sleep had become a luxury she couldn't afford. As twilight descended, her mind would stir to life, dragging her into a relentless loop of regret. "If I could just have one more chance," she whispered, voice choking with sorrow. Clutching a framed photograph of her boys, Michael and Steve, she traced the edge of the glass with trembling fingers, her heart craving the time when their laughter echoed through these walls.

The two boys had been everything to her, bright lights in a world that sometimes seemed unbearably dark. Michael, with his spirited imagination, had dreams of becoming an astronaut. Steve, the quieter one, had a love for painting that brought color to their lives. She could still see them running through the yard, wild and free, their laughter blending with the summer breeze. But that was before the accident, before the night when everything changed.

That night, Tracey's world fractured like glass underfoot. Panic surged as she replayed the events, her heart racing with every "what if." What if she hadn't let them go to the party? What if she had been there? What if she had taken their keys when they handed them over, inverting uncertainty into safety? Each thought clawed at her chest, brutally familiar yet impossibly distant. Reality had turned into a cruel game of chance, where fate had written a story that she could never rewrite.

Sighing, she sank into the couch, fighting back the swell of memories. The walls seemed to close in, whispering the possibilities she couldn't change. She felt as if she were caught in an infinite loop of time and despair. The stars outside twinkled softly, indifferent to her pain. "Why would you let this happen?" she cried out to the night sky, her anguish carrying into the emptiness.

But then, in the midst of her torment, a soft flutter caught her attention. It wasn't the wind or the creak of the old house; it was something far more ethereal. Tracey turned toward the window and noticed a small spider just outside. It was weaving a web, each strand drawing intricate patterns against the night. For some reason, in that moment, she felt a strange kinship with the creature. She watched as it meticulously crafted its design, resiliently moving along its thread, each movement a testament to life, despite the fragility of the web.

Tears blurred her vision as she considered the artistry of the spider's work, how each choice it made led to a creation so beautiful yet precarious, bearing the weight of intentionality. It struck her then—life was much like that web. It was a tapestry of decisions, some influenced by fate, others by the candles of agency she herself had the power to wield. Chances were irrevocable and woven without regard for her pleas, yet perhaps her late sons had woven their own tapestry too.

Tracey took a deep breath, and instead of drowning in the past, she felt a flicker of warmth in her heart. The boys would have wanted her to embrace life, to weave new paths through their memories. "If I could just have one more chance," she said softly, imagining them smiling down upon her, urging her to live, to love, to be free again.

Wiping tears from her cheek, Tracey picked up her sketchbook. It had gathered dust, neglected just like her dreams. But tonight, in that moment lit by potential, she began to draw. She poured her emotions onto the blank page, letting the memories of Steven's curiosity and Michael's creativity guide her hand. Each stroke was a tribute, an act of defiance against the shadows.

Night morphed into dawn, and as the sun broke over the horizon, its golden rays spilled into the room like hope inching back into her heart. She looked around, seeing the walls not just as reminders of what was lost, but as a canvas for what could still be. Tracey began to weave her own web, embracing not only the memories of her boys, but the possibilities of her future—a future that could still echo with laughter, art, and love.

In that web of life, she found herself anew, stitching her sorrow and hope into something markedly beautiful.

Chapter 6: Flying Again

The shadows thickened. Days turned to weeks, and Tracey could barely lift herself from bed. It was as if the entire world had turned into a muted gray, the vibrant colors of her life drained away, leaving only a desolate landscape behind. She found solace in the darkness, allowing it to cradle her like a long-lost friend, one that would not ask her to rise or engage with an unforgiving world outside her window. In this cocoon of gloom, she could close her eyes and succumb to the memories of her boys.

The laughter of her children, Michael and Steve, echoed in the corners of her mind—laughter so pure and infectious it could chase away any storm. She would remember their endless energy, Michael jumping on the bed while Steve spun in circles until both collapsed into giggles and exhaustion. But that warmth, like sunlight breaking through the fog, was always swiftly chased away by an aching, haunting shadow that reminded her of her loss—the fateful day that changed everything, haunting her like a specter that refused to leave.

Tracey wished she could turn back time, return to the moments before the accident—the call that shattered her world, the fragmented whispers of doctors, the despair thick as fog around her. They told her to be strong, to take it one day at a time, but how could she put one foot in front of the other when her heart was a barren wasteland? The world outside her golden memories felt like a prison, the walls built not of brick, but of grief.

For weeks, she could barely gather the strength to crawl out of her bed. Sheets long forgotten began to collect dust, now billowing hardly disturbed. Tracey barely noticed the sunlight filtering through the curtains or the delicate shadows dancing across her walls. She stayed wrapped in silence, feeling as though the world would forget her if she allowed herself to fade into the background. The house was still, save for the languid rustling of the wind and the occasional creak of the old wood, sounds that murmured like the whispers of her boys.

But beneath the blanket of sorrow, a flicker of life remained. The years she had spent nurturing them, watching them grow, were not all in vain. They had shaped her—made her stronger than she believed possible. Though enveloped in shadows, they had become her beacon. Each night, she would drag herself to their room, keeping the door ajar just enough for the memories to spill into her heart. Their toys, once cast aside after too many adventures, lay silent, inviting her to remember the joy instead of the loss.

One particularly heavy day, while lying in the suffocating silence of her room, a vivid memory emerged—Michael's dream of becoming a professional basketball player. She could picture the way his cheeks would puff with determination as he was preparing for games at his high school. That vision ignited a spark, one that shot through her like a comet crashing back to the earth. Michael had a friend named Landon on the team—a very nice, respectful friend as well as an awesome basketball player. She remembered Landon making a shot from one side of the court to the other. The crowd went crazy. Great memories.

Picking herself up after what felt like an eternity, she made her way to the living room. It was time to bring the colors back into her life, even if only a little at a time. She rummaged through a box collecting dust and pulled out a pair of worn, vibrant kites. A smile cracked her lips as she brushed her thumb over the faded fabric. She remembered the day they had flown them together, the echoes of their laughter heightening her sorrow, yet somehow pulling her closer to healing.

With trembling hands, she ventured outside for the first time in months. The sky loomed above her, an endless tapestry waiting to embrace the playful dance of the kites. Tugging them into the open air, she felt a rush of hope as the wind lifted them higher, swirling colors against the brilliant blue, mimicking the laughter that resided in her heart. Each tug on the string was a reminder that though shadows had thickened, light still penetrated.

Surrounded by the whispers of her boys that day, she knew that while their physical presence was lost, love lingered on. With each gust of wind, every colored tail soaring upward, they were with her, urging her forward—reminding her to breathe, to live, to fly again. Through the quiet acknowledgment of her pain, Tracey began to emerge from the cocoon of darkness, ready to let the warmth of the world in once more. And somehow, the shadows had started to lift.

Chapter 7: Finding Strength in Shared Grief

One afternoon, as Tracey scrolled through an online support group for grieving mothers, her heart was heavy with memories she had buried. Her fingers grazed over the screen, lingering on the words of others who had suffered unspeakable losses. For so long, she had told herself that she could battle her grief alone. She had wrapped her pain tightly in silence, believing that vulnerability was a weakness. But today was different. Something deep within her stirred—a hint of curiosity, a whisper of understanding. For the first time, she felt the faintest flicker of hope.

Tracey hesitated. The cursor blinked at her as if urging her to share, to be seen. She took a deep breath, a mixture of excitement and dread swirling within her, and began typing. "My name is Tracey, and I lost my son a year ago. Michael was 17 when he passed away and Steve was 12 but Steve was the older one. Michael is the middle child. Jaquan is the youngest." As the words poured out, the dam she had constructed around her grief started to crack. With every keystroke, she felt the weight on her heart loosen ever so slightly.

"I try to stay strong for my family," she continued, "but some days, it feels impossible." Those two sentences unleashed a torrent of emotion she had buried for so long. She wrote of the quiet evenings spent staring at Steve's empty room, of build-your-own antique cars and Michael's football gear all over the house. They felt like suffocating reminders, and the endless question of why. After pressing "Send," she sat in a silence that was both terrifying and liberating.

To her absolute surprise, the responses flooded in like lifelines tossed into turbulent waters. Each notification chimed like a bell of possibility. "You're not alone," one mother wrote. Another shared her own heart-wrenching journey, revealing that she had lost her daughter to a rare illness two years prior. "I know the dark corners of grief," she said, "but I've found light too." Tracey felt a surge of connection that made her weep.

Hours passed as she engaged with each reply, sending heartfelt acknowledgments back and forth, sharing laughter over cherished memories and tears over poignant losses. The mothers' words wrapped around her like a soft blanket, and in this virtual sanctuary, she began to feel the warmth of community. They celebrated small victories together and caught each other when days turned dark.

As evening settled, Tracey realized she had shared more of her soul than she had thought possible. In those many messages, she found solace in stories of resilience—about how lost loved ones had inspired lives to be lived fiercely, moments to be savored. Slowly, the flicker of hope within her transformed into a glowing ember, challenging the cold grip of despair.

Days turned into weeks, and Tracey continued engaging with the group. She found herself sharing not just her sorrows but also moments when she felt Michael's spirit around her. A butterfly that danced by her window, the smell of his favorite cookies wafting through the kitchen, or the way the sun's rays seemed to illuminate her path on particularly gloomy days. Each story she shared was met with understanding and compassion, each response offering her a glimpse of light.

One day, as she hovered above the fading screen, she decided to arrange a small gathering for the women from the group in a local park. With butterflies in her stomach, she typed out the invitation, not entirely sure how it would be received. To her delight, the responses were overwhelmingly positive. They were excited, each mother eager to connect in the tangible world, to embrace the rawness of shared grief that had blossomed online.

On the day of the gathering, Tracey arrived early, heart racing with a mix of anticipation and nervousness. When the first mother arrived, they exchanged warm hugs that spoke more than words could convey. One by one, they filled the park with the fragrance of coffee, pastries, and the sound of laughter punctuated by moments of vulnerability. They sat in a circle, sharing stories about their children, recounting precious memories, laughing as they recalled quirks and interests that had brought joy into their lives—joy that they had thought forever lost.

By the time the sun dipped beneath the horizon, Tracey realized that she was no longer standing alone in her grief. In this circle of understanding, she had carved a sacred space filled with shared love and loss—an unbreakable bond forged in the fires of suffering. As they released lanterns into the sky, each glowing light a tribute to their children, Tracey's heart swelled with gratitude.

In reaching out for support, she had not just found solace but a newfound strength to honor Michael's memory—a commitment to carry her love forward. Together, surrounded by understanding hearts, they breathed life back into their existence, wrapping their grief in compassion, and planting seeds of hope in the fertile ground of community. And for the first time, they were not just grieving; they were healing—together.

Chapter 8: The Courage to Heal

Tracey sat in the sterile therapist's office, the walls washed in calming shades of lavender and green, almost resembling a soothing garden in spring. Sunlight streamed through the large windows, spilling warmth across the plush, cream-colored couch. It felt like a safe cocoon, a stark contrast to the turmoil that raged within her. The tranquility of the space was a world away from the storm she'd been battling for so long.

Just weeks ago, the idea of stepping into a therapist's office had felt insurmountable. She had been wallowing in a sea of despair, too consumed by the weight of her emotions to even contemplate reaching out for help. But during her darkest moments, her friends rallied around her, lifting her up with words of encouragement and compassion. They reminded her that it was okay to seek assistance, that showing vulnerability was not a sign of weakness but an act of bravery.

Taking that leap into the therapist's office felt like surrendering to the storm instead of trying to navigate through it. And as she sank into the couch, the room filled with the scent of calming lavender essential oil, she felt a flicker of hope igniting in her chest.

"Tracey, you've shown immense courage just by being here," her therapist said gently, her voice soothing like a lullaby. "Let's take this one step at a time. What brought you here today?"

As these questions unfolded, Tracey's heart began to unravel. She could feel the knots in her chest tightening. She took a deep breath, and with it, the words tumbled out—the losses, the regrets, the uncharted grief that had taken up residence in her heart. The pain was palpable, constricting, yet freeing. Each emotion she acknowledged felt like peeling away layers of a long-held burden.

Through her tears, she spoke of her father's passing, how it had swallowed her whole, a void that echoed in her soul. She had never truly allowed herself to grieve, always pushing it aside for the sake of responsibility and others' expectations. Now, here in this gentle space, she began to learn the importance of giving herself permission to grieve. It was not a sign of weakness; it was part of her healing.

Days turned into weeks, and with each session, she faced the tangled emotions that had imprisoned her heart. They were not as easy to untangle as she had hoped. Some brought forth waves of sorrow that felt insurmountable, but others began to shimmer with the warmth of acceptance. Embracing her sorrow was akin to stepping into the light after being wrapped in a dark shroud for too long.

The therapist guided her through exercises that taught her to sit with her feelings, to observe them without judgment, and to express them in ways that felt authentic. Tracey found solace in writing—a cherished journal where she poured her emotions out onto the pages, spilling ink that captured her heart's raw truth. With each word, she reclaimed a piece of herself she had long thought lost.

Slowly, like flowers blooming after a fierce winter, Tracey began to transform. The process was painful, but it was necessary. She learned that facing her emotions head-on allowed her to move through them, not around them. It became her lifeline, connecting her to her past while illuminating new paths ahead.

With humility and newfound resilience, Tracey began to see the world through a different lens. She started volunteering at a local support group for those grieving, sharing her story, and whispering words of encouragement to those who sat in silence. She had once felt so alone in her struggle, but now she reveled in the empathy that arose when she connected with others.

Tracey's journey was far from over, but as she left the therapist's office one brisk autumn afternoon, the leaves crunching beneath her feet, she felt lighter. She turned her gaze upward, and for the first time in a long time, she smiled. The deep-rooted pain was still part of her, but it no longer defined her. Instead, it had become a testament to her strength and courage. With each step, she was less imprisoned and more free—ready to embrace the beauty of life, both in its joy and its sorrow.

Chapter 9: Rising from the Storm

One morning, Tracey woke up and felt different. Not healed. Not happy. Just… different.

Grief had been with her for a long time, like a shadow she couldn't escape. It was in every room, every thought, every breath. But that day, something small changed.

And for the first time in a long time, she got out of bed without having to force herself. Usually, she had to lie there, whispering to herself, *Come on, you have to get up. The kids need you.* But this morning, her body just moved.

In the kitchen, she made a cup of coffee. She stood there for a moment, listening to the silence. It was the same silence she had known for months, but it didn't feel quite as heavy. It was still empty, though. Michael's laugh wasn't there. Steve's voice wasn't calling from the other room. Two chairs at the table would always be empty now.

This was her reality: she still had children, and she had lost children. Both things were true, and both hurt in different ways.

She thought of Jaquan, her third son. He had lost his brothers too, but he almost never showed it. He stayed busy, always helping, always moving. He tried to be strong, as if he could fill the spaces Michael and Steve had left. Tracey could see it in his eyes, how much he carried, even if he never spoke it. It broke her heart all over again.

Her daughters each carried their grief in their own way. One cried openly, tears falling without shame. Another grew quiet, keeping her pain inside. Another laughed and pretended nothing had changed, until a memory hit her like a wave and she broke down suddenly. Tracey tried to hold them all, to comfort them all, but sometimes she felt like she was drowning herself.

How could she teach her children to grieve when she was still learning how to breathe without two of her sons?

Everyday life carried reminders. When she cooked lunch for the girls, she thought of Michael and Steve and their favorite meals. When Jaquan came home from school, she felt relief, then sadness, knowing the other two would never walk through the door again.

At dinner, they sat together. The kids argued over small things, shared stories from their day, and passed dishes around. To anyone else, it looked like a normal family meal. Tracey smiled, asked questions, and laughed when she could. But inside, she wondered, *"Where are my two sons?"* There was an empty space at the table, one she wished no one else could see.

After dinner, Jaquan helped her with the dishes. He was quiet, stacking plates carefully, until he finally asked, "Mom... are you okay?"

It was such a simple question, but Tracey felt its weight. Her son was grieving too, yet here he was, worrying about her. She looked at him with tears in her eyes and gave the only honest answer she could.

"I'm here," she said softly. Not "I'm fine." Not "Don't worry." Just: *I'm here.*

And he understood. In their home, those words meant: *I'm broken, but I'm still standing. I'm hurting, but I haven't given up.*

That night, one of her younger daughters came into her room, "Mama," she whispered, "do you love us?"

Tracey froze. "Of course I do, baby. I will always love you."

"But... you're so sad all the time. I thought maybe we weren't enough anymore."

Tracey's chest ached. Her grief had made her daughter question her mother's love. She pulled the child close, holding her tightly.

"Listen to me," Tracey said, tears in her eyes. "My heart is big enough for all of you. I'm sad because I miss your brothers. But that doesn't mean I love you less. You are enough. You've always been enough. My sadness isn't about you, it's about them being gone."

Her daughter cried, and Tracey cried with her. In that moment, they carried the pain together.

This was the hardest part of Tracey's new life: grieving for her sons while still mothering her living children. She had to balance her pain and her love, carrying both at the same time. Some days, she couldn't do it. On those days, Jaquan stepped in, keeping things together. They all learned too early that sometimes even mothers fall apart.

But other days, Tracey surprised herself. She made breakfast. She drove the kids to school. She listened to their stories, smiled at their little victories. She was still a mother, even when it felt impossible.

Yet the reminders were constant. Watching Jaquan play basketball reminded her of Michael, who had loved the game. Helping with homework reminded her of Steve, who had been so good with numbers. Every moment of joy carried a shadow.

But slowly, she learned something important: she could carry both. She could grieve and still love. She could be broken and still be present. It wasn't about choosing between her living children and the ones she lost. It was about holding them all in her heart, even when that heart felt shattered.

One afternoon, she sat outside, watching the kids play. Jaquan tossed a ball with his sisters, their laughter filling the yard. For a moment, Tracey felt peace. Not happiness, not freedom from grief, but a gentle peace.

Then the wave of sadness came again. Tears slid down her face as she thought of Michael and Steve. This time, she didn't wipe them away. Jaquan saw her and came to sit beside her. Soon, the girls gathered around too.

"I miss them," Tracey whispered.

"We miss them too," Jaquan said.

And so they sat there in the grass, a family still together, but missing pieces. Both whole and broken. Both complete and incomplete.

This was Tracey's new normal. Rising from the storm didn't mean going back to who she used to be. It meant learning to live as someone new, a mother who carried both life and loss.

Grief would always stay with her. But so would love.

She was learning to live in both worlds: to set the table for seven instead of nine, to celebrate birthdays while mourning the ones that would never come, to laugh again without guilt, to cry without shame.

It wasn't fair. It wasn't easy. But it was her life now.

And somehow, she kept going, for Jaquan, for her daughters, for Michael and Steve's memory. And, slowly, step by step, for herself.

Chapter 10: Letters to the River

Tracey sat in the circle of worn-out chairs, her heart heavy yet somehow lighter than it had been in months. The walls of the small community center were adorned with cheerful murals, vibrant flowers danced alongside gentle reminders of the beauty in life. Yet, those colors felt muted in contrast to the gray shadows that had enveloped her since that tragic day when she lost her sweet Steve and Michael.

The support group had felt like a last resort, a faint glimmer of hope in the abyss of her grief. The other women in the room wore expressions she had come to recognize—expressions of pain intermingled with flickers of resilience. As Tracey looked around, she saw not just reflections of sorrow, but mirrors of her own journey—a journey woven into the fabric of shared experiences.

"Today, I want us to share a memory of our children," said Linda, the group facilitator, her voice warm and inviting. Tracey felt a small rush of anxiety; the prospect of speaking felt daunting yet liberating. One by one, the stories began to unravel in the soft, muffled tones of remembrance.

Jenna, with her long hair pulled back tightly, spoke of her son who loved to build sandcastles. "He would insist on adding an entire army of toy soldiers to protect them from the waves!" she said, and a ripple of laughter passed through the group. Tracey smiled, picturing a tiny boy gleefully defending his fortress against the toiling tide.

Next was Sofia, who shared a heartwarming tale of her daughter's love for baking. "We never made it to the perfect cupcakes," she chuckled softly, her voice thick with nostalgia. "But we created the best mess together." The room erupted in gentle laughter, and for a moment, the weight of loss felt a little lighter.

When it was finally Tracey's turn, she hesitated, her fingers trembling as she thought of Steve and Michael. Taking a deep breath, she spoke of summer days spent in the park, Steve and Michael spinning in circles, her laughter ringing out like music. "She had this way of making everyone around her smile. It was like she had her own kind of magic," Tracey said, her voice steadier now, as she could feel the warmth of understanding radiating from the group.

As she shared, Tracey felt the threads of her sorrow weaving into something more—a tapestry of resilience. The tears that followed weren't solely from grief but also from the cathartic release of belonging. The camaraderie enveloped her in a comforting embrace, blurring the boundary between heavy heartache and hopeful healing.

After the meeting, they lingered a little longer, the bonds forged over shared pain beginning to evolve into friendships. Tracey found herself drawn to Jenna and Sofia, and they exchanged numbers, promising to meet for coffee next week.

"Together," Jenna said, her eyes sparkling with determination, "we'll remind each other to find joy again."

In the weeks to follow, their coffee chats turned into outings—mornings spent at picnics, afternoons volunteering at the local animal shelter. With each shared experience, Tracey felt lighter, as if each laugh, every touch of kindness, and all the sticky fingers from ice cream cones picked her up piece by piece.

One sunny afternoon, they sat in the park, the sun casting a warm glow on their faces. Sofia suggested, "Let's write letters to our kids. We can throw them in the river, sending our love downstream."

With a bittersweet smile, Tracey took out her favorite pen, and to her surprise, the words flowed easily. "Dear Steve," she addressed the first letter, and then, addressing the second letter, she wrote, "Dear Michael, I miss your laughter and your magic. But I'm starting to find my own again."

As she folded the letter and held it tightly in her hand, a sense of peace washed over her. The river next to them sparkled with life, and she stood with the others, joining in a poignant moment that felt like a tribute, a renewal of hope.

And as each letter was released into the water, carried away by the current, Tracey felt an unseen tether connecting her not only to Steve and Michael but to the fierce, loving community that surrounded her. In their shared moments of vulnerability, they were not just mourning together; they were embracing life together. "To new beginnings," she whispered, her heart buoyed by the strength of those who stood beside her.

Tracey realized that in the bonds they forged, the laughter they shared, and the courage found in vulnerability, she was beginning to heal—not alone, but in the embrace of a community that understood.

Chapter 11: Celebrating the Light

Tracey stood at the edge of the small, quiet park, watching the leaves dance in the gentle autumn breeze. Golden sunlight filtered through the trees, casting a warm glow around her as she clutched a tattered notebook to her chest. The air was filled with the sweet scent of fallen leaves and freshly baked cupcakes from the vendor nearby—a tempting reminder of the celebrations she had once enjoyed.

It had been a year since the unexpected losses of Michael and Steve. Michael had been a part of her life since 1996, and Steve since 1987, years that now felt both distant and achingly close. They were two pillars of her world, not just her children, but partners in adventure, laughter, and the complicated tapestry of her soul.

The grief had initially consumed her, wrapping around her heart like an iron vise. Each morning was a battle against the swirl of memories that threatened to drown her in sorrow.

But today, as Tracey stood in the park where they had spent countless hours, she felt a shift. Gradually, without realizing it, she had begun to pull the thread of her focus from the loss to the love that remained. The realization made her smile, and she flipped open the notebook, its pages filled with hastily scribbled notes, poems, and memories. Every word was a testament to the joy they had woven into her life.

She penned a new entry titled **"Celebration"**:

"Today, we celebrate. I can see us there—Michael's contagious laughter filling the air like music, and Steve's bright eyes reflecting the joy of a shared secret. They used to say life was too short for anything but celebration, and I can't let that wisdom slip away."

As she wrote, the memories surged forth, each one a bittersweet harmony. A memory suddenly sparkled, vivid and bright: Michael's birthday picnic last summer. They had laid out a checkered blanket on the grass, where laughter erupted over silly games and stories of their misadventures. Steve had shown up with a huge cake adorned with seemingly endless layers of chocolate, declaring it a "guilt-free indulgence" because calories didn't count on birthdays.

A chuckle escaped Tracey's lips, and she could almost hear Michael's animated voice echoing in her mind. On that day, nothing mattered beyond the shared smiles and carefree moments. They had celebrated life—not just the milestones, but the fleeting daily joys that made living worthwhile.

With newfound resolve, she let the memories wash over her, not as a source of grief but as rays of warmth in her heart. She would honor them, not through tears but through vibrant celebrations of their lives.

A plan began to take shape in her mind. She would throw a birthday gathering every year in their honor. It would be a day to reflect on the people they were, the memories they created, and the quiet strength they instilled in her. The annual birthday could serve as a testament to living fully, loving deeply, and celebrating passionately.

As she visualized the scene—a gathering filled with laughter, delicious cake, and friends sharing stories of her two favorites—she felt a surge of excitement. This would become an annual tradition, a lively reminder of love, appreciation, and resilience. They would toast to Michael's spirited humor and Steve's unwavering loyalty, perhaps even dress in colors inspired by their unique styles.

Tracey rose, the leaves crunching softly beneath her feet as she made her way back home. The notebook tucked under her arm was filled with plans for the birthday celebration: a gathering of friends and family, laughter mingling with the aroma of cake, and toasts echoing through the air. They would tell stories, watch the sunset together, and remember both Michael and Steve with joy.

Gradually, she had learned not just to hold onto their memories, but to fill them with warmth and gratitude, allowing the sharp edges of grief to soften into a gentle embrace. Tracey smiled to herself; she was ready to celebrate, to let love shine, and to carry their spirits in every joyful moment life would bring her way.

Chapter 12: Finding Life Again

Tracey stood at the kitchen window, gazing out at the barren trees swaying under the weight of winter. The world outside had grown gray and silent, reflecting the void she felt since the loss of her boys. It had been nearly a year, yet the ache in her heart felt fresh as morning dew. Each night, she nestled under the weight of heavy blankets, often haunted by echoes of the laughter that had once filled her home.

But there was a whisper inside her—a gentle urging—that perhaps it was time to step out again, to reclaim some semblance of joy. One crisp morning, emboldened by a flicker of determination, Tracey decided to venture into the world beyond her four walls. With a soft scarf wrapped snugly around her neck, she stepped outside, the cold air biting slightly at her cheeks.

Her first destination was **Winton Terrace, Ohio**, Michael's favorite place to socialize with his friends. Steve had passed away before they had moved to Winton Terrace. It wasn't an ideal place to want to hang out in, but as Tracey reminded herself, you cannot always choose where your friends live, nor judge them by their neighborhood.

With tentative steps, she made her way toward the familiar playground. The scene was a blend of chaos and joy; children dashed about, their giggles ringing like the sweetest music. For a moment, she felt an overwhelming wave of sorrow. But then a small boy ran by, his infectious laughter capturing her attention. It was then she realized—these children were not strangers; they were a reflection of her own boys.

Feeling their presence in the laughter of the kids, Tracey stood there, absorbing it all. It was as if their spirits danced among those lively little figures. Each playful shout that echoed through the park twisted and wove through her memories, wrapping around her heart like a warm embrace.

Day by day, Tracey returned to the park. With each visit, she ventured a little further out of her comfort zone. She started by bringing a book, reading under the sprawling branches of an oak tree, allowing herself to be both present and lost in stories. Other parents began to notice her, and soon, she found herself talking to the occasional passerby, sharing smiles, and exchanging childhood anecdotes.

The sun shone brighter as spring unfurled her arms, painting the world around with vivid greens and blooming flowers. With each warm day, Tracey noticed life transforming in many ways. She became acquainted with a woman named Lila, who shared her own tales of loss over steaming cups of coffee by the park's fountain. Together, they discovered that the weight of grief could begin to lift when carried gently—if not shared—among others who understood.

One beautiful afternoon, as the sun dipped in that fading golden light, Tracey sat atop a blanket, surrounded by children at play. With every burst of laughter that filled the air, her heart stitched itself back together, piece by piece. She felt the warmth of spring surrounding her—a promise that even after the harshest winter, life would emerge anew.

She closed her eyes for a moment, finding comfort in the harmony of jubilant sounds. For the first time in what felt like lifetimes, Tracey allowed herself to hope. The park, once a place of profound sadness, had transformed into a sanctuary—an oasis of healing.

And with every return, she found herself weaving into the fabric of life again, embracing the beauty of small moments and the joy that blossomed around her. The shadows of her loss would always linger, but now they were tinted with memories of laughter and love. In the depths of her heart, she carried the boys with her—forever intertwined within the laughter of children, forever echoing in the beauty of spring.

Chapter 13: Turning Grief into Purpose

Tracey stood before the mirror, her reflection a mosaic of resolve and sorrow. The faces of Michael and Steve haunted her thoughts—two sons lost to a world that seemed too heavy for them to bear. It had been one year since the tragic news shattered her reality, leaving a silence in their absence that felt insurmountable. In the wake of their passing, Tracey vowed to honor their memory. She decided to take action, channeling her grief into a purpose that could illuminate the darkness that had swallowed her children.

She signed up as a volunteer at a local suicide prevention hotline—a beacon of hope for those teetering on the precipice of despair. The office was modest, filled with comforting colors and soft lighting, designed to provide a semblance of safety in its embrace. On her first day, she was handed a headset, and with it, the promise of being a lifeline—one call at a time.

The first few hours were quiet, just the sound of her heartbeat echoing in the small room as she adjusted to her role. But soon enough, the phone rang, piercing the stillness like a cry in the wilderness. Tracey took a deep breath, recalling the laughter and joy Michael and Steve had brought into her life. She could almost feel their presence, urging her on.

"Thank you for calling," she greeted, her voice steady yet warm.

The voice on the other end trembled—a young woman named Lisa, her panic palpable. She spoke of feeling lost, of days that bled into nights without meaning, the gnawing pain of isolation. Tracey listened—really listened—her heart aching for Lisa, who felt invisible in a world that should have been vibrant.

With every call that followed, Tracey found herself enveloped in the stories of others—from the lonely teenager grappling with acceptance to the middle-aged man facing the shadows of regret. Each voice was a testament to the significance of connection, of simply being heard. The hotline became a sanctuary, offering not just words but a safe harbor to navigate the turbulent seas of despair.

As she listened, Tracey ventured to share pieces of her own story, her own moments of darkness. "You are not alone," she would often say, echoing a message she desperately wished she had conveyed to Michael and Steve. "I'm here with you." She felt their spirits with her, guiding her, as if they were proud of the path she had chosen. Each call morphed into a dialogue of vulnerability—a reminder that love and understanding could fuel the will to keep going.

One evening, as the sun dipped below the horizon, casting a warm glow through the office windows, Tracey received a call that lingered in her heart. It was a high school boy named Alex, whose voice quaked with fear. He spoke of being bullied and feeling like a burden to his family, battered by relentless waves of hopelessness.

Tracey listened intently as she felt the weight of his words. She offered him her ear, her heart, just as she wished she could have done for Michael and Steve. "Alex," she said gently, "remember, it's okay to feel lost. But it's also important to reach out for help. You don't have to carry this alone."

When they ended their conversation—Alex unburdened, still scared yet a little hopeful—Tracey felt a flicker of light in the pervasive darkness surrounding her past. Each time she hung up a call, a piece of her felt lighter—not because the pain was gone, but because she was helping to create a sense of hope where there once was despair.

Months passed, and every conversation deepened her understanding of the fragility of life and the power of empathy. Tracey organized talks at local schools about mental health, spreading awareness to those who might be locked in silence. She learned that the act of listening was sacred—an intimate exchange that could shift the tides for those hanging on by mere threads.

In the quiet hours before dawn, as she sat reflecting on her journey, Tracey would often think of Michael and Steve. She envisioned them looking down, smiling, perhaps even nudging her to keep going, to keep listening. Tracey turned her grief into a bridge that connected her to others in their darkest hours, crafting a legacy of honor that transformed despair into hope.

Though she could never bring her sons back, she honored them with every life she touched—a testament to the profound impact of simply listening and providing care. Each call became a reminder that even in the depths of despair, connection could make all the difference. In her heart, she knew that through her work, Michael and Steve were never truly gone; they lived on in the stories, the voices, and the hope sparked anew by each soul who felt heard.

Chapter 14: Then and Now

Tracey sat at the small kitchen table, her fingers curled around a mug of coffee that had already gone lukewarm. The house was still, so still she could hear the faint tick of the clock in the hallway. She looked around at the quiet, the empty chairs, the untouched counters. Everything was different now. Everything.

Two years ago, mornings were a rush of movement and sound. Michael darting through the kitchen, toast in one hand, juice in the other. Steve's calls lighting up her phone again and again before lunch, silly questions, jokes, just wanting to hear her voice. The air had been alive with laughter, with footsteps, with life.

Now the silence pressed in like a heavy blanket. On some days it suffocated her. On others it wrapped her in a strange kind of peace.

Her eyes fell on a photo lying on the table. The three of them at the county fair. Michael on one side, Steve on the other, cotton candy clinging to their fingers, all of them laughing under the summer sky. Back then, her biggest worry had been making it home before midnight.

"I didn't know," she whispered, her thumb tracing their faces. "I didn't know those were our last good days."

Back then, she was the worried mom. She stayed up late waiting for the boys to come home. She made big Sunday dinners. She fussed about the mess, the loud music, the dishes piled in the sink.

Now she would give anything to scrub those dishes again.

But something had shifted inside her too. Two years ago, she'd been a blur of work and motherhood. She didn't know her neighbors. She rushed through grocery stores with her head down, always somewhere to be. She had no time for herself, no time for anyone.

Today, she knew the names of people on her street. She volunteered at the hotline three days a week. She met Lila for coffee every Thursday. She wrote in her journal every morning — something she'd never done before.

The old Tracey had been surrounded by people yet felt alone. The new Tracey lived alone yet felt connected, in ways she couldn't have imagined before.

Just yesterday at the grocery store, she'd reached up to help an old man grab something from the highest shelf. He'd thanked her with tears in his eyes, saying no one had been kind to him in weeks. The old Tracey would have walked past without seeing him.

Loss had taught her to see. Pain had taught her to notice.

She drained the last sip of coffee, put on her coat, and headed out to work at the hotline. Driving there, she wondered who she might hear from today. Someone young and scared. A mother grieving. A stranger needing to know that someone, somewhere, cared.

The old Tracey's world had been small, her home, her job, her boys. It was a gentle kind of happiness, but narrow. She hadn't known how many people were hurting, how wide the world's ache was.

The new Tracey's world was larger now. Scarier. But also richer, deeper. She carried Michael and Steve with her everywhere, not as a crushing weight, but as a quiet guide. As reminders to love harder, listen longer, pay closer attention.

When she walked into the hotline office, a small card sat waiting on her desk. It was from Lisa, the first caller she'd ever helped. Inside were the words: "Thank you for saving my life."

Tracey smiled, and the ache in her chest softened. It wasn't the happiness she used to know. It was heavier, deeper, carved out of sleepless nights and tear-stained days. It was the kind of happiness that grows from surviving, from showing up, from learning to live with a broken heart.

She put on her headset and took a deep breath. The old Tracey would have been afraid of other people's pain. The new Tracey was ready, to listen, to help, to be the voice in the dark she wished Michael and Steve had found.

Outside the window, the sun was rising. A new day. A day to help someone find their way back to the light.

Chapter 15: The Weight of Grief

Tracey woke up on a Tuesday morning and couldn't get out of bed. Not because she was sick or tired, but because grief felt like a heavy stone on her chest. Some days were like this. The sadness came without warning, thick and heavy, making even breathing feel hard.

She stared at the ceiling, watching dust float in the sunlight. Michael would have been twenty-five today. She had forgotten until now. The guilt hit her like a punch. How could she forget her own boy's birthday?

Tears came quickly, hot and fast, soaking her pillow. She pulled the covers over her head, wishing she could disappear. This was the worst kind of grief — not the gentle sadness she could carry, but the wild pain that made her want to crawl out of her own skin.

Her phone buzzed on the nightstand. Probably Lila, wondering why she hadn't shown up for their walk. Tracey let it ring. She couldn't face anyone today. She couldn't be the strong woman who helped others. Today she was drowning in her own darkness.

Hours passed. The sun moved across the wall. Time slipped away, but grief didn't care about time or plans. Today it wanted everything from her.

She remembered the early days after the funeral, when people brought food, flowers, and kind words. Everyone had said the same things: "Time heals all wounds." "They're in a better place." "Everything happens for a reason." They were meant to comfort her, but they tasted like lies.

Time didn't heal wounds. It only taught you to live with scars. And if Michael and Steve were in a better place, why did she feel so alone? What possible reason could there be for taking two young men with so much life ahead of them?

Anger surprised her. She had been sad, broken, lost — but angry was new. Angry at the world, at herself. Angry at people who still had their children. Angry at mothers who complained about teenagers making messes or staying out late. She wanted to shake them and scream, "At least they came home!"

Mostly, she was angry at Michael and Steve. How dare they leave her? How dare they take away her purpose? She had built her whole life around caring for them. Now what was she supposed to do with all that love that had nowhere to go?

The guilt came rushing back. What kind of person was angry at her dead boys? What kind of monster was she becoming?

By afternoon, hunger forced her out of bed. She walked to the kitchen slowly, like an old woman, though she was only forty-three. She found some soup Lila had brought last week and heated it up. She could only eat a few spoonfuls. Even swallowing felt like work.

She wandered through the house, seeing ghosts everywhere. Michael's favorite chair by the window. Steve's jacket still on the coat rack. Their old gaming console, now covered in dust like a shrine.

The house felt like a museum of her old life. Everything was still there, but nothing alive anymore. She was the keeper of memories, protecting things that mattered only to her.

Her phone rang again — this time the hotline supervisor, probably wondering why she hadn't shown up. Tracey stared at the phone until it stopped. How could she help others when she couldn't even help herself? She felt like a fraud, offering hope to strangers while having none for herself.

She thought about the irony. She had become the kind of person she used to help — someone standing at the edge, wondering if it would be easier to let go. The difference was she knew too much now. She knew the signs, the danger. She wasn't there yet, but she could see the path, and it terrified her.

Evening came. She managed to eat a piece of toast and drink some water. Small victories. She thought about calling Lila but couldn't find the words. How do you explain that grief isn't a straight road from pain to healing? That it's more like a spiral staircase — sometimes you climb up toward the light, sometimes you fall back into the dark?

Her support group had talked about this. "Grief isn't straight," Linda had said. "Some days will be harder than others, even years later. That doesn't mean you're going backward. It means you're human."

But knowing something in your head and feeling it in your heart are two different things. Today, all her wisdom felt like lies she had told herself on easier days.

She found herself in Michael's room, a place she rarely went. The walls were still covered in his posters — bands she didn't know, movies she'd never seen. His bed was made, the way he left it. She had washed the sheets once, then stopped, afraid to lose his smell forever.

She sat on the edge of the bed and picked up a book from his nightstand. It was worn and bent, with messy notes in the margins. She couldn't read most of the words, but seeing his handwriting made her heart ache. This was proof he had dreams, thoughts, a life she had never fully known.

That's what hurt the most — not just that they were gone, but that she would never know who they might have become. She would never see Michael grow older or Steve build his own future. All those possible lives had been buried with them.

The darkness outside her window was complete now. She had lost another day to grief. Part of her felt ashamed. But another part knew this was necessary. You can't rush grief. It comes when it wants, and the only way through it is through it.

She made herself a cup of tea and sat in the living room, scrolling through old photos. There they were at the beach, sand in their hair. There they were at Christmas, fighting over gifts. Ordinary moments that now felt more precious than gold.

The pain was still there, and always would be. But sitting with it, not fighting it, made it a little more bearable. Grief wasn't something to fix. It was something to carry, like a heavy bag on a long walk. Some days the bag was lighter, some days it nearly broke you. But still, you kept walking.

Tomorrow she would get up, shower, and go back to the hotline. She would help others carry their bags for a while. She would be strong and hopeful because she had learned how. But today, she let herself be weak, lost, and human.

And maybe that was okay. Maybe Michael and Steve wouldn't want her to be strong all the time. Maybe they would want her to cry for them sometimes, to miss them so much it hurt, to love them so fiercely it left her breathless.

The love hadn't died with them. It had nowhere to go now except deeper into her heart, where it lived with the grief, tangled so tightly she couldn't separate them anymore. Maybe that was how it should be. Maybe love and loss weren't opposites but partners, dancing together in the space where memory meets hope.

She finished her tea and called Lila back. Her friend's voice was warm with worry and relief.
"I was worried about you," Lila said. "Bad day?"
"Yeah," Tracey whispered. "But I'm still here."
"That's enough," Lila said softly. "That's always enough."

And for tonight, it was.

Chapter 16: Two Worlds

Tracey stood at her kitchen counter, spreading peanut butter on a single slice of bread. Just one slice. Her hands still expected to make food for more, but now it was only her. The jar of peanut butter that once lasted a week now lasted months.

Her phone buzzed with a message from her sister, Sherrie: "Kids are driving me crazy today! Emma won't stop whining about her homework, and Jake ate the last of the cereal AGAIN."

Tracey typed back: "Sounds like a full house."

She didn't add what she was really thinking: *I would give anything for someone to eat all my cereal.*

This was her life now – living in two worlds at once. In one world she went to work, bought groceries, and spoke politely to people. In the other, she remembered what it felt like to have her house full of noise and life.

At work, people no longer looked at her with sympathy. They treated her like everyone else. In some ways it was easier. In other ways it felt like the world had forgotten.

At lunch, a coworker complained about her teenage son's messy room. Tracey smiled and nodded. Inside, she remembered Michael's messy room, how she used to scold him, and how she would give anything to see it messy again.

After work, Tracey drove past the high school. Teenagers poured out of the doors, laughing and walking in groups. For a moment, she thought she saw Michael's tall shape, Steve's walk. Her heart hurt.

Her calendar was empty now. No games, no curfews, no phone calls about being late. The freedom she once dreamed about now felt endless and hollow.

At the grocery store she carried a small basket while other shoppers filled their carts with family-sized food. In line, she watched a little girl ask her mother for candy. The mother gave in at last. Tracey stayed quiet, remembering what it was like to argue with children over small things.

Back home, she ate her simple dinner alone. On the news, a clip showed a school's homecoming game, students cheering in the stands. Tracey remembered sitting at games herself, sometimes distracted, taking for granted how precious those ordinary moments were.

Later, her friend Lila called. "How was your day?" she asked.
"Fine," Tracey said. It was true and not true. She had done what she needed to do, but she had also spent the day living in two realities — the world where she functioned and the world where she still grieved.

After the call, she sat in the quiet of her house, hearing only the hum of the refrigerator and the tick of the clock. Other homes on the street were full of noise, homework, and family life.

Tracey had lived in both worlds — the loud, exhausting, precious world with children, and the calm, organized, lonely world without them. Both were real. Both were hers.

Learning to live in both at once — that was her daily challenge.

Chapter 17: The Deepest Wounds

Grief is not a list you can finish. It doesn't move in neat steps. When someone dies by suicide, feelings come and go in a messy, confusing way. One moment you feel nothing, the next you are crushed. Then you might feel calm for a short time — and suddenly all the pain comes back.

Tracey learned this the hard way.

At first, denial felt like protection. Your mind refuses to believe the impossible. Yesterday they were here, laughing or asking about dinner. Today they are gone. The world feels unreal, like you are watching a movie about someone else.

With suicide, denial often turns into searching. You read old messages and replay conversations, looking for a clue you missed. You become a detective in your own life, hoping one small thing would change everything.

Anger comes next, like a storm. You are angry at yourself for not seeing the signs. You are angry at the world for being unfair. You may even be angry at the person who died. That anger is normal. It does not mean you did not love them. It means you are human and hurting.

Bargaining follows. You make deals in your head — with God, with fate, with anyone. "If only I had…" becomes a constant song. With suicide, these bargains turn into endless "what ifs." You imagine a thousand ways you could have helped. That thinking never ends because there are so many possibles.

Depression is deep and heavy. It is more than sadness. It is the crushing feeling that you missed the chance to help someone who was drowning. "I didn't know," you say again and again, and those words burn. Fear comes with this sadness. If you could not save your own person, how will you notice others in trouble? You become watchful and anxious, listening for signs everywhere.

Acceptance may seem impossible. It is not agreeing with what happened. It is recognising that it happened and learning how to keep living. Acceptance can bring understanding: suicide usually comes from pain that feels unbearable. People who die this way are not trying to punish others. They are trying to stop their own suffering. Knowing this may ease some blame, but it does not erase the pain.

The stages do not follow a straight path. You can be in denial in the morning, angry in the afternoon, bargaining at night, and feel a brief peace in between. This is normal. Grief moves in circles and waves.

If you lose more than one person or lose people close together, the pain becomes even harder. Loss piles up, and emotions mix in ways that make it hard to breathe.

Talking about suicide matters. Silence keeps stigma alive. When we speak openly about mental health, we give others permission to ask for help. If you worry about someone, ask them directly: "Are you thinking about hurting yourself?" Asking does not plant the idea — it can save a life. Many people who think about suicide are unsure; they want the pain to stop, not to die. A direct question shows you care.

Warning signs are not always clear. Some people hide their pain well. Others may suddenly seem better — that can be a danger sign. Watch for big changes in behavior, sleep, or friendships. Listen for words about being a burden, feeling trapped, or having no purpose.

Still, you must know this: you cannot control another person's choices. You can be kind, alert, and brave enough to ask hard questions, but you cannot save everyone. Mental illness is an illness. Sometimes people do everything they can and still lose the battle. That is not your failure.

Prevention is about building a culture where asking for help is normal. Treat mental health like physical health. Make reaching out a sign of strength, not weakness. Teach people how to listen and where to find help.

If you have lost someone to suicide, your pain is real and will likely always be part of you. But the pain can become bearable. You can carry your grief without being crushed by it. You can honor the person you lost while still living your life. You can use your pain to help others and to speak up for those who are suffering.

Healing is not "moving on." It is moving forward with the love you have and the lessons you learned. It is turning silence into conversation. It is holding on to hope long enough to find help. Suicide ends all the chances for things to get better — and things can get better, even when that seems impossible.

Stay. Talk. Ask. Listen. Help can come, if we keep reaching for it.

Chapter 18: Finding Purpose in Pain

The hardest part of losing someone isn't the first shock or the heavy sadness. It's the question that comes later, when people stop checking on you, when the cards and food stop arriving:

What now?

How do you keep living when the thing that gave your life meaning is gone? How do you go on when everything feels broken?

For many people who lose someone to suicide, the answer slowly becomes clear: you help others. Not because it fixes your pain or brings your loved one back, but because it turns your pain into something useful. It takes the worst thing that happened to you and uses it to stop someone else from going through the same thing.

This doesn't happen quickly. In the early days of grief, helping others feels impossible. You can't think of giving hope to someone else when you have none yourself. People who tell you to "find purpose" may feel like they don't understand your loss.

But with time, something changes. Your grief starts to live alongside other feelings. You begin to notice other people's pain. You recognize it because you've felt it too. You've been at the bottom, so you see when someone else is falling.

Moving from victim to helper isn't easy. Some days you can support others. Some days you can barely stand yourself. Learning when to step forward and when to step back becomes part of healing. You also learn to care for yourself, the way you wish your loved one had cared for themselves.

Working in suicide prevention can heal and hurt at the same time. Every story reminds you of your loss. But it also gives you a small chance at a different outcome — a chance to help someone else survive. You can't save your own child, but maybe you can save someone else's. You can't have the conversation you wish you'd had, but you can have it with someone who needs it now.

You learn an important truth: most people who are suicidal don't actually want to die. They want their pain to stop. They can't see another way out. Your role isn't to talk them out of dying but to show them there are other ways to stop the pain.

These conversations are different from normal ones. You don't tell them "it will get better" or compare their pain to yours. You listen. You believe them. You ask about their support, their reasons for living, their plans for staying safe. You don't judge. You hold space for their pain.

You also get training. You learn warning signs, risk factors, and how to act fast if needed. You learn to recognize dangerous words like "I'm tired of being a burden" or "I feel trapped." You understand that sudden calm after depression can be a sign someone has decided to end their life.

But your deepest training comes from your own loss. You know the guilt, the "what ifs," the weight of not being able to save someone you love. This makes you stronger and softer at the same time. You can connect with families, and you can offer real hope to people in crisis, because you've been where they are.

The work changes you. You become more alert to small signs in people's words or actions. You check in more. You ask harder questions. You talk openly about mental health, therapy, depression, and suicide. Some people find this uncomfortable. They think you're being dramatic. But once you've lost someone to suicide, you can't ignore signs anymore.

The truth is that talking about suicide saves lives. It breaks shame and stigma. It makes it safe for people to speak up before it's too late. When you model openness and vulnerability, others feel permission to do the same.

Prevention isn't just about answering crisis calls. It's about building a world where people feel connected and supported long before they reach the edge. It's about treating mental health like physical health — urgent, important, and normal. It's about better resources, more education, and leaders who make mental health a priority.

Losing someone also shows you that personal pain is linked to bigger problems — poverty, discrimination, isolation, lack of care. You realize you can't save everyone with one conversation. Real change also needs better systems and policies.

Even with all this, you will sometimes lose people. That is the hardest part. You try everything, and still, someone may choose to die. This does not mean the work is useless. Every life saved matters. Every person who steps back from the edge carries your loved one's memory forward.

You build a complicated relationship with hope. You know how fragile it is, but you've also seen it return. You've seen people rebuild their lives. You learn to hold both truths — that life is fragile and that healing is possible.

Finding purpose in pain doesn't erase the pain. Nothing can. But it gives the pain meaning. It turns loss into action. It honors your loved one by helping others survive.

This is how you live through the unlivable: not by moving on, but by moving forward. You take what you learned in the dark and use it to light the way for others. Every person you help, every family you keep whole, every life saved becomes part of your loved one's legacy — proof that even the deepest pain can be turned into something that helps the world heal.

Chapter 19: The Ripple Effect

When someone dies by suicide, the effects don't stop with their close family. The loss spreads outward like ripples in water, touching many people in ways that are often unseen. Understanding these ripples is important for healing – not just for the family, but for everyone affected.

The first ripple hits those who were there when it happened or who found the person. They often carry painful memories and images they never expected. They may blame themselves for not acting fast enough or not saying the right things. This also includes first responders – like emergency workers, doctors, or crisis counsellors, who already have heavy jobs and now carry even more emotional weight.

The second ripple reaches friends, classmates, coworkers, and neighbors. Even if they weren't very close to the person, they still feel shock, sadness, and confusion. Many ask themselves if they missed signs or could have done something to help.

In schools, the ripple effect can be especially hard. Students feel a mix of guilt, sadness, and fear. Some worry about "contagion" – when seeing or hearing about suicide increases risk for others. Teachers and school staff must find ways to honor the person while also keeping students safe and avoiding harmful messages.

In workplaces, the same challenges appear. Colleagues may feel unsure about what to say. Work may slow down as people grieve. Some become extra alert about others' mental health, while some pull back, afraid of saying the wrong thing.

Social media has added a new layer. Online memorials can give comfort, but they can also spread wrong information or unintentionally make suicide seem romantic or heroic. Comments may lead to other people sharing their own struggles, which sometimes turns into new crises. Digital memorials stay online forever, so the grief can feel fresh for a long time.

Mental health professionals often see more people after a suicide. Some people start therapy for the first time, trying to understand how someone could feel so desperate. This can reduce stigma about mental health, but it also puts extra pressure on already limited resources.

Families with teenagers or young adults may become more watchful, worried about their own children. Conversations about mental health suddenly feel urgent. Some families grow closer by talking openly; others struggle with fear and stress.

Religious communities face their own challenges. Older teachings about suicide may not match modern understanding of mental illness. Leaders often wrestle with how to comfort families while staying true to their beliefs. Congregations may respond differently – some offer full support, while others struggle with judgment or confusion.

The economic ripples are often forgotten. Funerals, lost income, therapy, and medications all cost money, adding financial strain to emotional pain. Communities sometimes raise funds, but this can feel either supportive or overwhelming for grieving families.

Healthcare workers may also struggle. They might have treated the person before their death, leaving them with questions about what more they could have done. Emergency staff see the immediate aftermath and can become either numb or overly anxious about missing warning signs.

Law enforcement officers are often at suicide scenes. They must balance their investigations with sensitivity toward the family, all while handling their own emotions. Many communities now use crisis intervention teams to help.

The media plays a big role too. Responsible reporting can help educate and reduce stigma, but sensational stories can increase risk for vulnerable people. With social media spreading news so quickly, controlling harmful messages becomes even harder.

Healing a community after suicide takes effort. Support groups for people who have lost someone to suicide create safe spaces to share experiences and build understanding. These groups can include not only close family but anyone affected.

Education also matters. Programs that teach mental health awareness, suicide prevention, and crisis skills can help people feel less helpless. These programs work best when they're ongoing, not just short-term reactions.

Sometimes positive changes come from tragedy. Communities might build better mental health services, schools might add more counselors, and workplaces might offer employee assistance programs. These changes don't erase the loss, but they can prevent future tragedies and honor the person's memory.

Some communities create memorials or prevention projects in the name of the person who died. These can help people grieve and make a difference, but they must be handled carefully so they don't send the wrong message.

Everyone heals at their own pace. Some recover more quickly, others carry their pain for years. There's no set timeline for grief.

Recognizing the ripple effect helps communities respond better. It shows that support must reach beyond the immediate family and include everyone affected. It also highlights the need for easy access to mental health help.

Most of all, knowing about the ripple effect validates everyone's feelings. The coworker, the neighbor, the student from another class – their grief and worries matter too. Suicide affects whole communities, and healing must involve everyone.

Though suicide loss spreads pain, it can also spread awareness, compassion, and change. Communities that face the full impact together can heal better and work to prevent future tragedies. Suicide prevention is not just the job of professionals or family members – it's a shared responsibility.

Chapter 20: Reading the Signs

The question almost every suicide survivor asks is: *"How did I miss the signs?"* This thought comes with heavy guilt, as if noticing more or doing more could have changed the outcome. The truth is not so simple. Sometimes there are clear signs. Sometimes there are none at all. Knowing this is important for both prevention and healing.

The clearest sign is when someone talks about suicide directly. If a person says, "I want to kill myself," "I wish I were dead," or "You'd all be better off without me," those words must be taken seriously. They are not just drama or attention-seeking. Many people who die by suicide have said something like this before, though often it was not noticed at the time.

But not all signs are so clear. Some are small changes in daily life. A person might pull away from family and friends, sleep too much or too little, stop eating well, lose interest in things they once loved, or stop taking care of themselves. A student may stop trying at school, or an employee may stop doing their work well. Mood changes also matter. Sadness and depression are warning signs, but so is suddenly looking calm or happy after being deeply down. That can sometimes mean the person has made a decision to end their life and feels relief in it.

Giving away special belongings or getting affairs in order can also be signs. Drinking more alcohol or using drugs more often is another danger, because these lower control and make a person more likely to act on dark thoughts. In today's world, signs can show online too. Posts that sound like goodbyes or talk about death can be cries for help. Still, social media can hide pain—some people look happy online while suffering inside.

It is also true that many of these behaviors can mean something else. A teenager may pull away just because they want independence. An adult may lose sleep because of work stress. Someone might give away things just because they want to clean their space. What matters most is when you notice several changes together, or when a person seems very different from how they usually are.

Looking for signs helps, but it is not enough. Often, by the time signs are clear, the person may already be in crisis. That is why prevention also means creating safe and caring spaces where people can ask for help before they reach that point. Schools, workplaces, and communities can all help by teaching coping skills, building strong connections, and reducing shame around mental health.

One of the most powerful things you can do if you're worried about someone is to ask directly. Saying, "Are you thinking about hurting yourself?" or "Are you thinking about suicide?" does not put the idea in their head. Instead, it opens the door for them to speak honestly. If the answer is yes, thank them for trusting you, take them seriously, and help them connect with professional support.

A safety plan can also help. This is a simple plan the person makes with support. It includes their own warning signs, ways to cope, people they can call, and reasons to stay alive. It may also mean removing or locking away dangerous items, like guns or large amounts of medication. This does not remove all risk, but it can slow things down and give time for help to arrive.

After a suicide attempt, follow-up care is very important. The risk is highest right afterward. Regular contact, ongoing treatment, and steady support can greatly lower this risk. Technology also helps today—crisis text lines, apps, and online support groups are always available.

Suicide prevention is not only for professionals. It is something we all share. Communities can train people to notice signs and respond with care. Schools and workplaces can take action to protect mental health. Even the media has a role to play, by reporting on suicide in safe and responsible ways.

Suicide rarely happens because of just one reason. It usually comes from many struggles joining together, like mental illness, stress, loneliness, and easy access to lethal means. Helping with even one of these lowers the risk. Real prevention means working on many of them at once.

The goal is not for everyone to be an expert, but for people to care, to notice when something seems wrong, to listen without judgment, and to guide others to help. Sometimes, the most powerful thing you can do is simply to be there.

Suicide can be prevented. It takes effort, care, and community. Most of all, it takes the belief that everyone has a role to play in helping others feel seen, supported, and hopeful, even in their darkest hours.

Acknowledgments

Thank you, Dr. Kevin Eggerman, for saving my life. Your compassion and expertise gave me the tools to survive my darkest days and find purpose in my pain. This book exists because you showed me that healing was possible.

Tracey Crump

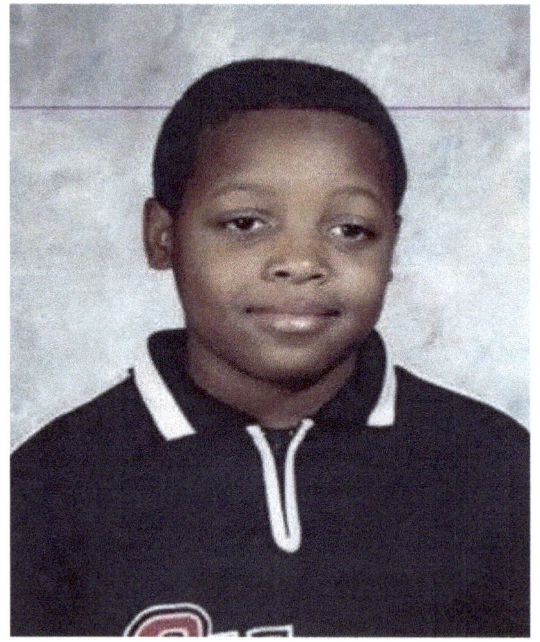

Michael and Steve I carry you in my spirit.